The Birth of A Union

The Legacy of Noridean McDonald

by

Davida Russell

Bloomington, IN   authorHOUSE®   Milton Keynes, UK

AuthorHouse™
1663 Liberty Drive, Suite 200
Bloomington, IN 47403
www.authorhouse.com
Phone: 1-800-839-8640

First published by AuthorHouse 7/3/2007

ISBN: 978-1-4343-1001-9 (sc)

Printed in the United States of America
Bloomington, Indiana

This book is printed on acid-free paper.

Table of Contents

DEDICATION

THE SWITCH

There is a switch that lies dormant within each of us

When danger threatens

There is a force that calls us to duty

There is a need within us all to perpetuate good

change

Let us answer the call

Let us make the stand

Let us call out with hope

Then let us find the elusive Switch of change.

We salute Noridean McDonald for reaching out,

for the change that she made for the County

transportation workers of OAPSE Local #744

(Russell, D. 2006).

Davida Russell

President OAPSE/AFSCME Local #744/AFL-CIO

Introduction

One determined person can make a difference that can change conditions in a workplace, a community, and even a country. Noridean McDonald made a lasting difference in her workplace. What motivated one woman bus driver to lead the fight for change in the working condition and compensation for transportation workers, and what remains of her legacy in the workplace today?

"The Birth of a Union," OAPSE[1] Local #744, gives a glimpse into the life journey of Noridean McDonald and her legacy to the transportation workers of the Cuyahoga County Board of Mental Retardation and Development Disabilities (CCBMR/DD) in Cleveland, Ohio. This story describes Noridean's struggle to form a union for the County transportation workers, her court fight to establish the employer for that union, and the contracts she negotiated that have represented CCBMR/DD transportation workers and their former vendor for the past 27 years.

While a majority of OAPSE Local #744 members have 20 or more years of service with CCBMR/DD, the majority lack knowledge of the history of Local 744's fight to come into existence. Most members do not realize if Noridean McDonald had not taken a stand on behalf of the transportation workers, their lives would not be the same. Members take for granted seniority rights, vacations, health care benefits, and

---

[1] Ohio Association of Public School Employees

competitive wages, to name a few, because these members were not part of the original struggle.

The purpose of this paper is to allow the members of OAPSE /AFSCME[2] Local #744 to understand who started the union, why it was necessary to start a union, and how the union was formed. This paper informs affiliates, sister unions, and current active members how one person can make a difference. When pulling workers together in unity, the lives of many are changed.

To understand the extraordinary changes that have occurred and to anticipate the even more dramatic changes that lie ahead, union members need to look back at the main features of discontent underlying Noridean's motivations, undermining the very fabric of the relationship in the workplace between management and employees. For instance, the reality that seniority did not count motivated Noridean and propelled her into the forefront of tackling workplace issues. This spark is reminiscent of a statement by Thomas Jefferson: "We mistrust those who think they already have the answers when we are still trying to formulate the questions" (Alvin and Heidi Toffler 1994-1995).

Noridean's clarity of vision brought with it a new degree of stability and a sense of self in the workplace at a time none could be found. Noridean came of age in the midst of extreme polarizations of power, as labor and management grappled for control of the main levers of transformation that would soon characterize dominance in manipulating how the fragmented workplace would be reorganized for the future.

Noridean McDonald started out her adult life as a young housewife of a General Motors union worker who was a candidate for councilman for Ward 27 in Cleveland, Ohio. As the mother of two daughters, she primarily worked only for extra amenities to enhance her family lifestyle. She held various short-term, non-union jobs and paid very

---

[2] American Federation of State County and Municipal Employees

little attention to the plight of others who depended on this type of employment for survival. It was not until she accepted employment with CB Transportation, a vendor of the County, that she began to include herself in the day-to-day function and organizational makeup of her place of employment. After various experiences, Noridean felt she found a job she could label as a career. She found her niche, a job that provided decent pay and flexible hours so she could still fulfill her duties as wife and mother. Little did she know the series of events and choices would lead her to a place one might call the Twilight Zone!

This paper shares a story of struggle and provides a sobering lesson into expectations and what it takes to cultivate and empower a movement at its grass roots beginnings. This paper illustrates that for OAPSE Local #744, the quality contracts achieved, the great working conditions, and the respect from the employer that the transportation workers enjoy today are a direct result of Noridean McDonald's struggles and her successes in organizing the transportation workers to form a union. It is in these successes and policies that Noridean's legacy lives on today.

Literature Review

"Let no one be discouraged by the belief that there is nothing one man or one woman can do against the enormous array of the world's ills—against misery and ignorance, injustice and violence …Few will have the greatness to bend history itself; but each of us can work to change a small portion of events, and in the total of all those acts will be written the history of this generation…

It is from numberless diverse acts of courage and belief that human history is shaped. Each time a man stands up for an ideal, or acts to improve the lot of others, or strikes out against injustice, he sends forth a tiny ripple of hope, and crossing each other from a million different centers of energy and daring, those ripples build a current that can sweep down the mightiest walls of oppression and resistance."

Senator and Attorney General Robert Francis Kennedy, South Africa, 1966

(Acquired through The Arlington National Cemetery Archives).

What would it be like if the masses had no voice and a powerful few ruled with no challenge? How loud would the thundering silence be? Who would step up against all odds and be the umbrella of equality and justice? Only a rare few! It is regrettable that such conditions exist for blue-collar workers in a non-union setting, and the workers still suffer the pain of injustice and inequality. It is in times like these that rare individuals hear the cry for help. They come from all corners of the globe. They often make themselves available to harm while only seeking what's right.

Over the course of history, time has witnessed the sacrifice of these few for the betterment of all. Sadly we often see that so much is left to be done. Here we examine individuals who demonstrated to the world that their actions, commitment, and sacrifice made a difference. These are the people who have sent forth that tiny ripple of hope that has taken down the walls of injustice.

This is the study and the stuff that legends are made of, from histories theorized in George G.M. James's *Stolen Legacy* with Egyptian, Greek, and world mythology. There are various texts and stories of individuals making a difference, to the modern documented, historical chronicles rooted in scientific and archeological recorded facts, of individuals standing up for something they believe in. Their impact was felt by millions. This paper shares the experience of an individual who is like many others who have made a difference and changed the lives of many, while providing sources, data, data retrieval, interviews, and associated informational awareness and support.

This story of Noridean McDonald contains interviews and the retrieval of particular communicated facts or circumstances expressible in an exacting monotonic set of values, for the service of a purpose, an idea, a beginning of the theory of one person making a difference. In choosing to include not only the perspectives shared include but are not limited to those of Noridean McDonald. Through many resources, the reader will learn of Mrs. McDonald's efforts to overturn a set of values that had no place in a civilized work atmosphere, where rules of engagement should be in place for all concerned. Noridean's legacy is not the world stage of events but the ripples of the first stone cast.

Several familiar cases exist where an individual cast this symbolic first stone. A tribute to individual presence, leadership, and organizational work always adds to the collective's critical empowerment and growth periods of civilized man with slow leaps forward to embrace and hold dear greater freedom, equality, and justice. Dr. King's Herculean efforts from 1960 to 1961 in Albany, Georgia and Birmingham, Alabama led to the showdown in the Freedom March from Selma, Alabama to the state's capital of Montgomery. As referred to in William Roger Witherspoon's *Martin Luther King, Jr....To The Mountain Top,*

> *"All of these conditions were the fuel for violence and riots. As the social psychologist Kenneth Clark has said, it is a surprise only that outbreaks were not experienced earlier" (King, 1968, p.12)* from his book *The Trumpet of Conscience.*

Crystal Jordan (Norma Rae), union and labor activist turned leader, held the line and inspired and encouraged the reluctant, despite various forms of retaliation through lack of job promotion while being ostracized by peers in a minimum-wage cotton mill factory job. She orchestrated a shutdown of the mill, resulting in a victory for the union, and conceded to its demands that shaped and led a movement. All the big business efforts failed in the end to stop her, and she individually made a difference. It's time for the young people to consider that a living legend is a woman or man with the simple courage of Crystal Jordan, the courage to stand up for UNION stated in the artic union (*Standing tall with a living legend: unknown, from NALC real September 2003*).

Rosa Parks's personal and shared informative and enlightening journey caused her, as one individual, to be a catalyst and poster child of the birth of a movement. A recipient of the Eleanor Roosevelt Woman of Courage Award, Mrs. Parks shares the frustrations and successes with all the trappings of mystery and drama in *"They've Messed With the Wrong One Now"* from her book *My Story.*

> *"She had no army behind her. The law was against her. Only a few people knew her name. But Rosa Parks's individual act of courage and determination on Dec. 1, 1955, in Montgomery, Ala., ultimately changed a way of life, moving the nation closer to fulfilling America's founding principles, rooted in equality, liberty and the intrinsic value of every person"* (Unknown, from the Washington Post 10/26/05)

The influence of one person's victories, with all of their limitations and struggles, exists in this enormously complicated time in history — a great moment of history!

Despite being less known than the aforementioned leaders, Joseph P. Rugola began his career setting a path in and for unionism, in the state of Ohio. Mr. Rugola had a quiet start, leaving his humble roots as a union staff representative and activist to becoming the current head of OAPSE/AFSCME Local #4 union of Ohio. As executive director, he brought the union from 26,000 members to over 38,000 members, from bankruptcy to financial stability. Mr. Rugola has dedicated himself and is leaving his personal fingerprint upon the union and the political framework of Ohio.

Mr. Rugola was the first major supporter of the newly elected governor in Ohio. He has taken OAPSE/AFSCME Local #4 from the poor house to the state house. As was shared in an interview with State President Jo Ann Johntony of OAPSE/AFSCME Local #4, Mr. Rugola is truly one individual making a change, making a difference in how we act, perceive, and live as union members.

The film *"The Power of One"* features an all-consuming epic journey of triumph of the heart. It is the true tale of one man living by the words that one person really can make a difference. Peter Philip Kenneth Keith known as (PK), the son of an Englishman born in Africa, overcomes terrorism by the apartheid system (the Afrikaners who were Belgian, Dutch and German descendants) aimed with his family views of justice and equality. PK rises to the challenge when he brings multiple African tribes together in peace in a prison camp and earns their respect. He is honored with the title of "Rain Man," the bringer of peace. He wins the hearts of the tribe members, encouraging them to go against all odds in order to win freedom and dignity. PK went on to co-found an underground school system to teach black South Africans how to read and write as a means to gain equality, respect, and dignity in South Africa.

Around the world the struggle continues to gain human dignity and equal rights for all people. Change can come from the power of many but only when the many come together does that power become invincible. Other great individuals and their stories are sampled and referred to in the compilation of this paper. In addition, specific interviews, books, videos, movies, and articles mentioned and influencing the content and outcome of this assignment can be found in the bibliography.

The subject topic contains research elements on background informational readings, recorded material viewing, and quotes of the noticeable among us whose personal involvement in a crisis acted in struggle to create and mobilize a resistance structure inclusive of leadership for equal recognition and rights, to make a difference in the success of that mission for the masses. Using all phases of the multimedia available these individuals gained the unlimited use of available knowledge and different opinions to form ideas, methods, and an approach theory to connect with subject/subject matter in the quest of this goal. This vicarious gain of insight is through imagined participation in and of the experience of others, backed by witnesses, facts, and documented evidence and results.

Study Results

The study of Noridean McDonald's struggle demonstrates that the individual and the events are shaped by the constantly evolving notions of human rights and justice as perceived by civilized cultures and laws and their resistance against change, timed with their pursuit of change against the status quo in a flawed system of equality. A movement, an individual, and an idea are propelled by a new conspicuous conscience of mankind, designed for mankind by mankind. It is only when all elements of success align themselves for change that change occurs.

"A people who cannot remember their past are condemned to repeat it."

-George Santayana (1863-1952), poet

Methodology

The study included direct interviews with Noridean McDonald, active and retired rank-and-file members, as well as CCBMR/DD management staff who were directly affected or influenced by the birth of the union from 1979 to present. The author used the direct face-to-face interview technique to collect the information. This technique was chosen to validate the story of the union, as some of the original members and management continue to work for CCBMR/DD transportation service. Thirteen interviews were conducted. All interviews were open-ended; a tape recorder was used with permission from the interviewees. Four follow-up interviews were conducted. Three potential interviewees were unavailable due to being retirees who moved out of Ohio. Nevertheless, the participation rate was 80 percent, a high number because the members were accessible at a common work location. Interviews were limited to one hour which included both positive and negative recollections of the union's development and growth.

Interviews were followed by collecting and reviewing Local #744 contracts negotiated under the leadership of Noridean McDonald and contracts negotiated after her retirement in 2004. This assisted in identifying the legacy she left behind for the transportation workers. A comparison of contracts was drawn by a review of all contracts, their specific contractual language, and what provisions remained consistent throughout the existence of the Local. These data illustrate a consensus of information to determine the benefit of Mrs. McDonald's influence.

This was followed by research from the United States Government National Labor Relations Board Archives in Washington, D.C., to locate documents pertaining to the certification of representative of the Local union and documents from the court proceeding where Noridean McDonald had been subpoenaed to testify. Also, research into the records of OAPSE/AFSCME Local # 4 AFL-CIO was required to locate the charter of the union. In addition, I consulted a VHS tape from 1999, covering the 20th anniversary of OAPSE Local # 744. Research concluded with an interview with Mrs. Karen Houston Gee, the first OAPSE Local #744 field staff who walked the journey with Noridean McDonald to form OAPSE Local #744.

Examination of various books, biographies, newspapers, websites, and films such as *"Norma Rae"* and *"The Power of One"* were used to provide examples of how the power of one determined person can make a difference in the lives of many in any setting.

The Early Years

Noridean McDonald grew up on the north shore, of Cleveland, Ohio, a fantastic land of opportunity for many African-Americans migrants from the southern United States in the 1940s and '50s. This land offered a new start for many and a first beginning for others. The U.S. had become the envy of the world of manufacturing. The American Dream was in full bloom. There was a sense of purpose, a sense of being, and a sense of pride about "Made in America." The generations that paved the way taught Noridean to be loyal and to fight a good fight, and that all of the labors and trials would be rewarded by the grateful nation as a whole. Further, Noridean learned that would translate into equality and justice for all the undereducated, the blue-collar educated, and the college ranked. In America anything was possible as long as one kept one's eyes on the prize.

During the 1960s and '70s, a lot changed in the fabric of the blue-collar lifestyle. Upon reflection, one of the most truthful and accurate word combinations that described the north coast industrial region of the U.S. for Noridean is the affectionate term "the Rust Belt." Where once stood mighty machines of progress and envied factories of production now stands abandoned and neglected hulks of industry. The Rust Belt was Noridean's world; this was the hand that fate had dealt her. She was well aware of the cultural, political, and industrial changes going on.

Open the door to the pathway back to the moment, the mindset, and the reality of the year 1979. This is the year Noridean McDonald began her journey as a blue-collar worker to end the injustice of herself and her coworkers at CB Transportation. To provide insight on these times is a snippet from (*Remember When 1979*):

Double-digit inflation strikes the United States as prices rise 13.3%

The U.S. Government orders deregulation of oil companies

A serious gasoline shortage leads to long lines at the pumps

The average income per year is $17,533.00

The cost for a new house is $58,099.00

A new car costs $5,758.00

The average rent per month is $280.00

Tuition to Harvard University is $4,850.00 per year

Gasoline is 86 cents per gallon

Fresh ground hamburger is 90 cents per pound

Milk is $1.92 per gallon

Eggs are 48 cents per dozen

A movie ticket is $2.00 each

The best actress award goes to Sally Field for her work in the picture Norma Rae

Jimmy Carter is the 39th president of the United States

January 1979: Jimmy Carter proposes that Dr. Martin Luther King's Birthday be a holiday

February 1979: Ronald Reagan announces his candidacy for president in New York

A city that once cradled the mid-western blue-collar worker was Cleveland, Ohio. Like Detroit and Flint, Michigan, Cleveland provided much in the way of the American Dream. It was not too large a city and yet not too small a city in which to raise a family. Cleveland was a major marketplace, very significant in heavy industry such as steel production, automobile production, and commercial and house construction, with many support industries that thrived in the Rust Belt's heyday.

The winds of change were beginning to blow in 1979. It was the beginning of the end for the blue-collar workers who worked in the private manufacturing industries. The steel mills were in trouble and starting to downsize, the automobile industries began laying off workers, and the construction industries began to take a downturn. There is no easy way to describe the taste, the feel, and the emotion of the moment except to say it definitely was not a run-of-the-mill year for Noridean McDonald. Visit the places, the people, and the events that have shaped and defined OAPSE Local #744.

The Birth of a Union

It is 28 years since the day Noridean McDonald went on her crusade to organize the union for the Cuyahoga County transportation workers. It is the story of every man and woman in the workplace who needed to make a difference to improve every condition. Not for personal gain, satisfaction, or revenge against any person or any system did Noridean take up the gauntlet. She was introduced to the world of confrontation and conflict by those who would take advantage of a situation strictly to vanquish and disenfranchise a worker with less education than a high-school graduate and no professional assistance such as a labor union.

Noridean McDonald began work in transportation with Hogan's Transportation in 1971. From the time of her employment with Hogan's Transportation until the union came into existence in 1978 and 1979, the history of her employment was dotted by the change of transportation management companies on three different occasions. The first two times the company changed hands was hardly noticeable, and jobsite conditions did not change. The transition was very smooth. The workplace as a whole retained the integrity, policies, and practices they had long held, along with some added benefits. The third company had control of the transportation services in late 1978 through early 1982. When CB Transportation took over management, Darrel Courtney and Company sent in a staff of supervisors that seemed determined to change everything they possibly could. The new management implemented all new policies and procedures without regard for past agreements and grandfathered-in practices, such as seniority rights and the biding process for summer work.

The 175 workers, including approximately 52 percent African Americans and 48 percent Caucasians, struggled with adversity and hardship under the new company. The transportation workers were used to better treatment from past vendors of the County. Dave Systems, the California-based company that ran the transportation department from 1975 to 1978, based its employee relations practices on the idea that if you did not want a union, then treat your employees like they have a union: with respect, dignity, and fairness. Dave Systems lost its bid (Appendix 1) to run the transportation department to CB Transportation, not because CB Transportation was better but because the contract bid was cheaper. This was reflected in CB Transportation's poor people skills and management performance.

With employment in Cleveland starting to fail, no one was hiring in the private manufacturing industries, large or small, and the working population began to turn toward the public sector for fair jobs for blue-collar workers. As unskilled laborers, the population of the employees was comprised of those in their first jobs, housewives that needed to add income to their households, young adults fresh out of high school, folks without a high school diploma, and some just passing through. In this economic climate the workers did not want to jeopardize their employment with CB Transportation. Although their wages were only $3.60 per hour, the equivalent to $10.00 per hour in 2006 (according to the Bureau of Labor Statistics' inflation calculator), the workers depended on this income for their daily living expenses (BLS 2006). The job with CB Transportation was the sole source of household income for some workers. Many workers felt they could not take a chance on becoming unemployed.

Fear in the workplace is no joke. It allows employers to push and bully their employees to the limit of human tolerance. When this happens the employees can lose big. They lose their dignity, then their pride. Only when one has nothing left, does one tend to fight back.

CB Transportation came from Cincinnati, Ohio to set up business in Cleveland with the employment mentality and practices that workers were to do what they were told with no questions asked. Based on interviews with employees at the time, this company was very racially motivated and minded when it came to employee management relations in the workplace. Retired Assistant Operation Manager Louis A. Kish reflected on some of the practices and intimidation methods Bill Wolf, managing director, used to control the workers. Mr. Wolf kept a baseball bat visible in his office at all times. Whenever he decided to speak to the employees, he frequently used the "N word." Mr. Wolf stated, "There are two kinds of Negro people: the Black people and the 'N word' people." He addressed the Caucasian workers as two kinds of people as well: "the white people and the white trash people." His common phrase was, "When you speak to dogs you have to speak quietly and carry a big stick." To further entrench his leverage of control in the workplace, for example, on pay day he would always have a fellow who he referred to as his "bodyguard" escort him to the bank to pick up the payroll. This was some dramatic show of power to further dominate the workplace. The bodyguard dressed in black leather, wore many gold chains, and had a mean attitude, reminiscent of some Hollywood B-list movie about gangsters. The strange point of this behavior is the payroll was in the form of paychecks, not cash. Mr. Wolf seemed to perform this routine in an attempt to create an atmosphere of who is the boss and who is the employee — the basic good-old-boy mentality.

Members recall a practice that attracted attention and raised a red flag in the eyes of many employees: the change in unemployment policies. Many workers did not have enough seniority to bid for a summer route, a time when client enrollment was drastically down from winter levels. Past practices allowed for the employees who could not secure a summer route to claim unemployment during this layoff period, which is when Mr. Wolf came in. The next major concern was a policy implemented to change the seniority rules. Management began to let some of its favorite people and employees with little or no seniority gain preferred shifts and routes with total and flagrant disregard to a more senior employee's position.

The employees felt they were a responsible and effective work force that produced positive results for the clients they served. The traditionally healthy and productive workplace was disappearing. It seemed the company had made up its mind to get rid of or change all ways, practices, and policies that had already been established. For Noridean it became very hard and unbearable to get up and face going to work, not knowing what changing forces would be against them that day. The employees felt they were a responsible and effective work force that produced positive results for the clients they served.

One day in 1978, during these trying times, Noridean McDonald's fight started. Noridean's coworker and friend Ophelia Brock, a single parent with six children, came to work very upset. She was having problems with her children and had gone into the manager's office to request a leave of absence to deal with her personal family issues. The company gladly granted her this leave, and when the time came to return to work, the company denied her request. They claimed there was no work for her, despite the fact there were new employees with less than two months of service filling in for her and others who were on a leaves of absence. This was the "straw that broke the camel's back." The entire work force was upset and angered because they knew if the company succeeded here with total denial of employment rights, who would be the next one the company would come for?

Noridean McDonald started talking to two other trusted coworkers and friends. Idell Bunton and Beartrice Jordan spoke about and discussed the situation that faced them. They needed to stop this kind of behavior by the company. They needed to explore what unionization could provide for them, but no one among them knew anything about the process and procedures necessary to begin. Noridean began to talk with friends, relatives, and other bus drivers and monitors who belonged to existing unions, who could share information about how unions work. She also checked the libraries, newspapers, and magazines for any information she could find.

After a private meeting before work with Idell and Beatrice, Noridean was driving her route and came to the corner of Wilson Mills and Richmond roads, where she stopped to wait for the traffic light to change. A bus pulled up alongside her bus. Noridean smiled and waved at the other bus driver, and the bus driver returned the gesture. Noridean decided to take advantage of the moment. She opened her door and gestured for the other driver to open her window, which she did. Noridean asked whether she belonged to a union at the place she worked. Her reply was yes. Noridean yelled, "Who?" As the light changed and she proceeded on, she shouted out the name "OAPSE!." When Noridean returned to the bus garage that day she informed Idell and Beatrice of her encounter.

A few of days later on her route Noridean made contact with a second bus driver, this time a male. She got his attention the same way. He stated the union he belonged to was OAPSE. In a week's time, Noridean stopped and met five different bus drivers. Each said their union was OAPSE. The last driver she met in the same fashion suggested if their routes intersected the following day at the same intersection she would give her the phone number of her OAPSE field representative. When she returned to the bus garage that next day, she informed Idell and Beatrice about the phone number of the field representative she had acquired. They were curious, supportive, and suggestive of her perusing the information they needed to become more informed about the possible choices and possible directions available. After a complete understanding of the events and possible results that might result from this contact, it was agreed Noridean would reach out that evening to make contact with the OAPSE representative.

Noridean and Ms. Houston played phone tag for a few days until Ms. Houston left her home phone number on Noridean's answering machine. When Ms. Houston and Noridean finally connected, they discussed their individual abilities and concerns about the road they might soon embark on. By the end of their conversation, Ms. Houston assured Noridean she could help, and that the time was right for a union in their particular workplace for their particular circumstances. Armed with this information, Noridean carried the facts that Ms. Houston could help and that the job would be hard, long, and undercover. The two received the new information with apprehension but were very optimistic about the need to move forward. Noridean also encouraged the two friends to join her at a meeting she had arranged with Ms. Houston. The meeting was to take place after work at the McDonald's Restaurant on Noble Road in Cleveland Heights, Ohio. This would be the first face-to-face meeting with a real union representative.

Noridean was nervous about this encounter, but as the leader of this insurrection she could not let it show. Noridean encouraged her two friends to join her at this meeting to assist her in being able to deliver all of the concerns and needs of their workshop, and welcomed their input and the scrutiny of a person who soon might change their world forever. At the meeting Ms. Houston listened and took notes. By the conclusion of the first meeting, Ms. Houston promised to do further research and meet with them as soon as she had some information and a plan of how to proceed.

Through their conversations over the time period of Ms. Houston's investigations of their case, Noridean and Ms. Houston discovered they had a lot in common. They even lived in the same neighborhood. Once this fact was discovered, Noridean arranged for the next meeting to take place at her house. Noridean knew her coworkers would be more receptive and cooperative to new ideas, new forward thinking, and a new mindset of conduct and plans if it took place in a familiar and comfortable atmosphere. At this meeting, the core group of Noridean, Idell and Beatrice met with Ms. Houston. She began to dissect what it would take to begin the process of bringing a union on board. She explained it would not be all roses, cut and dried, and user friendly. Ms. Houston told Noridean of the courage, dedication, and sacrifice it would take and the kind of actions she would depend on and need from Noridean and her coworkers in order to see this thing through. She went on to explain the types of actions she would bring to the table to help them bring this matter to a swift conclusion. The first thing she requested from Noridean was that she gather 50 percent plus one in the form of signature cards by the members requesting a union body of representation.

The next day, Noridean, Idell, and Beatrice secretly began a campaign to distribute and secure the needed cards and signatures under the very noses of the transportation company they worked for. They needed to keep their activities as discrete as possible because by now the company had proved to the membership that harassment and intimidation was their preferred method of dealing with the work force.

Noridean turned her home into the forward battle headquarters of the movement. She did all of it at her personal expense, including the production of flyers, using her personal vehicle, and donating her time and effort. She even had a second phone line added in her home so she could make contacts to encourage her fellow coworkers to join the movement. Noridean held weekly meetings and information banks to make union information available to those coworkers unfamiliar with a union structure and to those aware and interested in the new and proposed direction of a united body of workers. Noridean educated the coworkers by phone, word of mouth, and by distributing literature.

The number of necessary signature cards was quickly reached. Ms. Houston could then petition the company into a serious series of discussions and dialogue concerning the overwhelming and convincing vote of faith in the use and need to unionize their workspace. Next, they formally petitioned all parties involved of the people's will to unionize and to negotiate a contract. By law the die had been cast, and now they were a union shop. However, Ms. Houston needed to formally organize the body of workers into an accepted and legal force with the rights and due course afforded to them by law. This process took Ms. Houston three weeks.

Ms. Houston arranged a place for the new union to meet: the Amalgamated Textiles Union Hall, located between the 25th and 27th blocks of Payne Avenue in Cleveland, Ohio, which was 43 blocks from the workplace and approximately a 20-minute drive. This meeting would be the first union meeting of the new OAPSE Local #744. On July 3, 1979, the order of business involved the election of officers. This was necessary for all concerned to be able to bring this matter to the forefront. At this meeting Noridean McDonald was unanimously elected to become the first president of OAPSE Local #744 (Appendix 2). Noridean became the mother of her union's birth. The other positions were filled by the attending membership at large at this meeting. Now they could proceed forward under the watchful eye of Ms. Houston.

Beatrice and Idell chose not to run for an elected office, but both women chose to become part of the first negotiating team.

With an elected administrative body in place, Ms. Houston petitioned the employer for the right to negotiate a contract. They soon found out neither CB Transportation nor the County wanted to embrace the ownership and responsibility of the union. Neither Ms. Houston nor Noridean could make an appointment with CB Transportation in an effort to begin negotiations. After CB Transportation continued to ignore the workers' rights to negotiate as a bargaining unit, Noridean nervously prepared herself to use all means necessary to fight and win for the union. Noridean had enough of this behavior from the management, so she called an emergency union meeting to update the members. She explained how the management was doing everything possible to interfere with the contract negotiation process. Noridean then asked the union members for a vote on measures to stimulate movement by the management to enter into true negotiations. Noridean called on the members to take a strike vote in case a strong message was needed to get the company's undivided attention, if they remained stubborn and uncooperative. The strike vote was taken and her request was met with total support. As a unified body, they voted to use a strike as a means to achieve their goals. Noridean and Ms. Houston could now move to the next step if CB Transportation continued to resist.

With full support from the membership and a strike vote in hand, Noridean and Ms. Houston went back to CB Transportation to make an appointment to set up a schedule for negotiations. CB Transportation informed Ms. Houston and Noridean that they had no plans to talk or negotiate with them, as they did not recognize the union nor were the workers employed by CB Transportation. They claimed the workers were employed by the County. Noridean and Ms. Houston went to talk to the County about the discussion they had with CB Transportation concerning the allegations that the County was their employer. Sure enough, the County disagreed with CB Transportation and claimed CB Transportation was the employer. Noridean and Ms. Houston informed the membership of this claim and the need to go on strike.

Although OAPSE only had 15,000 to 20,000 members in the state of Ohio at the time, the state union did give Ms. Houston full support for a strike. After Noridean delivered the news to her coworkers/membership, she contacted Ms. Houston and asked how to proceed with the strike. Ms. Houston replied, "This strike will be my very first one!" Noridean looked at her in fear, but they could do nothing but laugh. However, the lack of experience in the participation in a strike gave them confidence to proceed in a romantic fight for justice.

This romantic notion was soon tainted by the stark reality of a long, hard fight. By the time these feelings surfaced, they had become battle-tested veterans dedicated to victory. There was no room for fear. It was time to choose a battle site. They selected William Pat Day Center, one of the County centers where CB Transportation had routed summer client transportation. Turnout on the first day was over 150 strong. The strategy adopted by OAPSE and Ms. Houston was to keep Noridean visible to her membership but shielded from any acts that would be deemed detrimental to the cause and strike. Through past strike experience OAPSE knew CB Transportation, like many other companies, would target the leadership to break a strike. The strike was just the beginning, and the new union could be quickly demoralized if their leader was eliminated from the struggle.

Noridean and Ms. Houston managed the organization and proceeding of the strike from a bus shelter in front of the William Pat Day Center, in front of the main activities. The first day of picketing proceeded without a hitch. From Noridean's perch she could direct the action and movement of the picketers to be in the most effective positions. She employed the "sit-in" style of protest. The protesters sat and blocked the entrance to the parking lot, which forced some of the hired yellow cab drivers and private transporters to abandon attempts to deliver clients to the Center. The more determined private transporters coordinated their efforts to deliver the clients to the Pat Day Center with the Center's teachers and staff. Their tactics was to park down the street and escort the clients on foot up the sidewalk to the edge of the picket line. Then they would pass the clients up and over the heads of the seated protesters into the waiting hands of teachers and staff members.

Roderick Speed, a mechanic with CB Transportation, said, "While some transporters were handing off clients to the Center's teachers and staff, some picketers took it upon themselves to smear petroleum jelly upon the windshields of the parked vehicles causing the transporters the problem of having to clean their windshields before they could leave the area." The petroleum-jelly smeared windshields gave the transporters something to think about when they had to return to the Center for further pick-ups and deliveries of clients. Despite limited success by the private transporters and staff of the Center, that day Noridean and her coworkers effectively and peacefully disrupted the transportation of the clients being delivered to the Center. Noridean, Ms. Houston, and the membership viewed their first encounter as a success. This strengthened the resolve of the membership and galvanized them into an effective force.

Over the next few weeks many scenes played out involving the strikers on the picket line. Roderick Speed recalled finding a coworker hiding in a row of hedges along the route to the Center. After coaxing her out of her hiding place, he discovered she had stockpiled stones, rocks, and bottles to use to stop the vehicles from attempting to deliver clients. The strikers on the picket line needed to be encouraged that this type of protest would hurt more than help their cause. All during the strike Noridean would quietly move among the union members to rally them together and remind them to keep their focus. After early successes, OAPSE contacted the news media. Media companies sent crews to monitor the progress of the strike and present it on local television and in newspaper articles. After receiving a black eye from the media, CB Transportation arranged for the Cleveland Police Department to deploy officers to control the strike line. There were exaggerated charges of destruction of property and threats of bodily harm and creating an unsafe environment around the William Pat Day Center. Rumors spread of police interdiction, and the membership grew nervous about jail and what measures would be taken to support them, despite having full support of the community, including the local labor unions and the families of the clients they serviced. Some families of the clients chose not to send their students to school to show their support. Noridean and Ms. Houston moved through the line of picketers reassuring them that OAPSE was there in support, and they had lawyers standing by to handle any situations that might arise. With no strike fund available and no financial support, to Noridean's surprise, not one person crossed the picket line to go back to work. They were strong and united.

Noridean had to constantly monitor any mischief that was happening and intervene where possible to maintain the focus of the union's strike. The non-violent and non-confrontational approach was proving to be community friendly and a positive method and Noridean did not want the members to abandon it. "There must not be any violence. We must remain in positive control. We must not be labeled. They must not portray us in a bad light and create the mindset to the public that we cannot be negotiated with," Noridean would remind them.

Despite her best efforts, members did get arrested due to the heightened emotions of the moment. None of the arrests resulted in injury or abuse because of the time Noridean spent on coaching the conduct of the membership. Noridean and Ms. Houston acknowledged that this was the first time they had gotten to know a bail bondsman on a first-name basis, and they hoped they would never have that pleasure again.

As if the day-to-day operation and coordination of a strike were not enough, Noridean and Ms. Houston continued to pursue a course of trying to end the trouble and the strike. Noridean spent many hours in communication with members, during the day as well as at night on her family's time. She would often travel to both garages, on the Westside and on the Eastside of town, once or twice a day to check, assist, and inform members of developments. The report remained the same: management still refused to discuss the matter with the union. Due to case-related brainstorming with OAPSE lawyers, court requests, and appearances to rescue members arrested on the picket line, there never seemed to be enough time in a day.

The strike continued through the summer and well into the winter. Attendance at the strike line continued to be quite strong despite the start of a slow decline. As the weather turned colder some members began to build small barrel fires to keep warm while on picket duty. They began to use the fire barrels to keep warm so they could stay on the picket line and keep the pressure up on CB Transportation. The police showed up and stated that Cleveland fire ordinances did not permit open fires in this manner. In order to circumvent the law, Noridean came up with the idea of using the fire barrel as barbeque grills to help the members keep warm. As long as they continued to keep some type of food cooking, no ordinance was broken. This idea was a big hit with the members, and the bleak atmosphere turned festive. They began to cook, eat, and enjoy themselves as if it was the middle of a July 4th celebration.

As weeks passed the cookouts of steaks, ribs, Italian sausages, and pork chops gave way to beans and hotdogs. Noridean became disheartened and worried for her members' well being. These were the times that truly tested the resolve of Noridean and the union.

Noridean recall at one point during those dark hours, when attendance was dropping, one of her Westside members single handedly held a Westside-targeted strike location alone with his motorcycle and his big dogs. Noridean called Al Spitznegal her "rebel without a cause who found a cause!" It was individual acts like Mr. Spitznegal who helped Noridean keep the strike alive.

Noridean remained a strong leader to the local but secretly cried every time someone mentioned their bills were getting behind or their children needed something. It was so upsetting for her to know that some of her members' spouses did not fully support them and their struggle. She could do nothing but hold the line with her head held high.

After continually being stonewalled by their employer, Ms. Houston filed a complaint with the National Labor Relations Board requesting they intervene in the dispute, and arranged that the issue be decided by the court system. Because the County and CB Transportation each denied they were the responsible employer of the transportation service unit, Ms. Houston had no one entity or corporation to bring to court for a swift resolution. While CB Transportation signed the paychecks, Ms. Houston decided to take both the County and CB Transportation to court to let the court system sort the whole matter out.

The court date was set for December 14, 1979. Noridean McDonald and 12 other bus drivers, monitors, and mechanics were subpoenaed to court in downtown Cleveland by Judge John F. Lenehan on behalf of the National Labor Relations Board. They were to testify in the matter of CB Transportation Services, Inc. Case No. 8-RC12009 (Appendix 3) to help the court determine who was their employer.

On the scheduled day of court Noridean found herself the lonely employee in a court room, face to face with CB Transportation's lawyers and staff, the County's lawyers and staff; and one OAPSE lawyer, Ms. Houston. The 12 coworkers subpoenaed to court were no where to be found, and it was vital to the case to have their testimony heard in court. Now Noridean became frightened and troubled about whether there would be a successful conclusion. She knew she was on the hot seat, and her job was in danger. She wondered if she would be fired or left unprotected. Noridean could not understand what happened to her coworkers when they knew the consequences of not responding to a subpoena. She later learned that CB Transportation threatened to fire any employee who appeared in court.

After such a great start to her campaign and all the encouragement that went along with it, she found herself in a very lonely place with no support. Noridean looked at Ms. Houston shaking and questioned, "Where is everyone else?" The bravery Noridean showed by not running out the courtroom doors that day made the fight worth it all. If she fled, the judge would have dismissed the case and the fight would have been in vain.

Ms. Houston addressed her concerns and guaranteed Noridean that she could not be released from her job for her involvement with the union. Ms. Houston informed Noridean that no one could take action against her because the courts had the last word in resolving the problem, and until the courts decided, she would be immune to harassment in any shape or form.

At this point of the court hearings, the judge stated smiling! "she was neither fish nor fowl, she did not belong to anybody" because neither body acknowledged responsibility as the primary employer. Two days of testimony began. The County claimed that the company, CB Transportation, was the employer, and they paid CB Transportation to run the transportation unit. CB Transportation claimed they were only the managing force. They stated they were a private organization not covered under Ohio employment laws or under the National Labor Relations Act. As managers they were strictly hired for organization, operation, route preparation, employee pay distribution, and employee records purposes only. After the County and CB Transportation gave their depositions, Noridean was called to testify. She knew she must remain strong in the face of this setback and feelings of abandonment. The judge questioned Noridean as to which of the two companies she worked for. She told the judge she really did not know but explained the County owned the buses, bought the fuel for the buses, stored the buses, and owned but leased the buildings that CB Transportation operated out of. Also it was in these buildings that the employees reported to work each day. In addition, the County provided CB Transportation the funding to meet the required weekly payroll.

The County responded to Noridean's testimony with the claim that the parents of the clients call CB Transportation for client schedules and pick-up and drop-off times for their special needs students. This is also where parents call and voice their complaints, concerns, or to even communicate their compliments of the services provided. Concluding the County's testimony, Ms. Houston whispered and asked Noridean if this line of testimony was in conjunction with what she experienced on an everyday basis at the job site. Noridean responded with a quiet but resounding "no"! "No, everything came from the County," she told Ms. Houston. To be sure to include all possible avenues of success, Ms. Houston asked Noridean if she could prove it, and Noridean said "yes!" Ms. Houston asked the judge for a short recess to be able to provide information that would support and legitimize Noridean's claims.

The judge granted them a recess period to bring any additional evidence and information that might be useful to the case. Noridean and Ms. Houston discussed the facts of their precarious position; they were floundering in the wave of a successful campaign mounted by the opposition. It was "do or die time," and all the cards needed to be on the table in order to win. Ms. Houston and Noridean discussed what type of evidence she had. Noridean informed her that some of the bus drivers were also parents of the special needs students they served, and they could testify that everything came from the County. While Ms. Houston went to the law library to pursue another angle, Noridean went to the pay phone to call Carolyn Jack, a bus driver and parent of a special needs student.

Fortunately, Carolyn Jack answered the phone. Noridean went on to explain the situation and asked Carolyn if she could come down to the court house to testify. Carolyn replied, "Yes, but I have my son and Betty Worley (a bus monitor) with me. Can I bring them along with me? Betty will gladly watch my son while I testify." Noridean informed Ms. Houston of the conversation and she replied, "By all means bring them!"

The courts reconvened. Carolyn completed her testimony by confirming Noridean's account of who she thought truly controlled and ran the day-to-day operations of the transportation services unit in which she was employed. The judge requested of the parties any further evidence that should be considered in this case. The County and CB Transportation rested their individual cases. Ms. Houston stepped forward to present her final evidence, some important facts that were over looked by the opponents to the union. She reminded and challenged the judge on how the laws governing interstate commerce included the employers of the transportation unit. Ms. Houston cited the law that stated the purchase of buses that total the amount of $50,000 falls under the Interstate Commerce Laws. This went hand in hand with the laws under the National Labor Relations Act. She brought evidence that proved the County had recently purchased two buses at a price of $35,000 to total $70,000, which clearly represented them as the true owners and operators of the transportation unit under question.

The court fight was finally over. The judge determined the County was the true employer for all concerned parties. The transportation workers had an employer and were recognized as a union. After the determination was made, the County directed CB Transportation to call off the strike and to represent them in negotiations with the new union in good faith in accordance with the court's decision.

As the strike was finally over, the transportation workers reported to work the very next day. Ms. Houston petitioned the National Labor Relations Board for union certification of representation status for the transportation workers of OAPSE Local #744. On March 10, 1980, OAPSE Local # 744 received certification of representation from the National Labor Relations Board (Appendix 4) along with an application for their charter with the Ohio Association of Public School Employees to represent approximately 175 transportation workers (Appendix 5, 6). On March 25, 1980, the Ohio Association of Public School Employees hereby approved and certified OAPSE Local #744's chapter name as the Cuyahoga County Adult Education Chapter of the Northeast District of Ohio (Appendix 7, 8, 9). Ms. Houston became the first appointed union representative of the newly certified OAPSE Local #744. Then, new and unexpected troubles began.

The management staff for CB Transportation, who was to negotiate with the union on behalf of the County, refused to follow through with their responsibilities. CB Transportation ducked and rescheduled over ten meetings with President McDonald and her negotiating team over a two-month period. They denied them the right to have their field representative present at negotiations on three separate occasions. When they did show at four of the meetings, they made outrageous demands and refused to accept any offers placed on the negotiation table by the union. Soon it was quite clear CB Transportation had no intentions of negotiating anything with the union, and they would not honor anything they agreed on. The union and CB Transportation made only four tentative agreements in a two-month period, such as pay checks, payroll error, work week, and dues deduction.

The labor laws and the mandate set down by the judge required that negotiations be done in a fair and proportionate manner. Noridean hoped for a smooth transition into becoming a union, but this was not the case. Noridean petitioned the County for help. After speaking with the County, the County directed CB Transportation to negotiate a fair contract with the union in accordance with the law or they would lose their contract with the County.

Noridean, Ms. Houston, and the negotiating team fought hard for months, page by page and detail by detail to get to a contract that would be fair to the company and one the members could live by. Months of negotiations and 28 pages later, on September 1, 1980, OAPSE Local # 744 finally had a contract agreement with CB Transportation. Members rejoiced over the increase of pay from $3.60 per hour to $4.04 per hour, along with a back-to-work rate of an additional 20 cents per hour for each individual. In addition, a seniority-rights clause was established:

> *"The principle of seniority as hereafter defined shall prevail. Seniority shall be defined as the length of time a regular Employee has served in the transportation department providing service to clients of the Cuyahoga County Board of Mental Retardation and serving in classifications covered by this bargaining unit as computed from the Employee's most recent date of hire to perform transportation related services" (Dourgherty, D., Houston, K. & McDonald, N. (1980, 1983, Pg.12), from the contract Agreement between CB Transportation Services, Inc. and the Ohio Association of Public School Employees.*

The goal of honoring seniority was the primary reason the transportation workers sought a union. They rejoiced over the long nights and weekends of successful negotiation. Little did they know CB Transportation did not care if they had just negotiated a contract; they were still determined to have things their way. Someone said "that book meant nothing to CB Transportation." They continued to give the workers hell. However, with the new contract, the employees now had rights under the National Labor Relation Act; the law was on their side. During the next two years, OAPSE Local #744 filed over 125 grievances, 125 won by the union; and the union arbitrated 36 cases, 35 won by the union.

OAPSE Local #744 members established themselves as a union that would not back down. The County discovered that CB Transportation was not honest in billing the County for their services, and the financial discrepancies began to grow. As the mismanagement of the negotiated contract between the union became evident, the County could no longer keep CB Transportation as one of its operating vendors. The County hired CB Transportation to manage and operate the transportation department because they were not familiar with running a bus operation. Little did the County know they would operate the transportation department as referee between the union and CB Transportation. Growing tired of financial discrepancies, mismanagement of the contract, refereeing the fights with the union, and the cost of the lost arbitrations, on September 1, 1982 the County terminated CB Transportation's contract in order to operate their own transportation department (Appendix 10).

Noridean's Legacy

Over the course of time, Noridean's path to creating a union inspired and touched union members as well as County administrators. It was recognized by both sides of the work force that Noridean "had the courage and the tools, and knew how to use them, to bring about change." During the stressful times as well as the good times Noridean created an atmosphere of trust and cooperation in her workplace. She remained a lady and a representative of the union with a cool head and a professional demeanor. Although many members and administrators think Noridean held the union office as president for many years, she held the office of president for only one term, the equivalent of one year. Noridean felt the members needed to take ownership of their union. The tools she provided them to protect themselves in the workplace would need to be used by everyone. So Noridean stepped away from the role as leader of OAPSE Local #744 in 1981. That said, she continued and remained chief negotiator and chief shop steward until the day she retired in 1999.

For 28 years, Noridean McDonald kept the foundation and integrity of the first contract she negotiated with CB Transportation and the County. From this initial contract, Noridean established the following: seniority rights, bidding recall, ongoing bid procedure, bid notice requirements, summer assignments, employee rights, non discrimination, grievance procedure and arbitration, steady pay checks, check-in, extra minutes, overtime, rotation of extra trips and overtime, pay schedules, work schedules, work segments, right of refusal, driver duties, and fringe benefits such as holidays, vacation, insurance, and sick leave. Policies that were established in this initial contract still exist and play a key role as the building blocks for the successful operation of the transportation department today.

The foundation created under Noridean's leadership remains in use as the blueprint of OAPSE Local #744's negotiated contracts. More recent contracts have seen additional amenities and compensation packages. Since her retirement Noridean has been called in as a consultant during OAPSE Local #744 negotiations as the historian and founder of the union. Today Noridean holds onto negotiation records and other records of the beginning of the union.

From the outset in 1979, when the fundamental fight for the union began, there were 175 transportation workers. When the union was recognized in 1980, the population of transportation workers had grown by 25 employees. From 1980 to Noridean's retirement in 1999, the CCBMR/DD Transportation Services hired over 150 new employees. From 1999 to the present, employees have come and gone through retirement and attrition and the loss of government funding. Yet OAPSE Local #744 — now OAPSE/AFSCME Local #744 — currently represents over 200 members and is growing.

Conclusion

After the interviews and study into the story and legacy of Noridean McDonald, it is my conclusion that working people (the transportation department at CCBMR/DD) developed a since of pride and dignity for what they found in becoming a part of the labor movement: a Local, a union, strong and united.

Noridean was president of a Local union for only one term (one year) but was so involved that members and administrators believed for over 29 years (until the day of her retirement) that she held a union office. In addition, the solicitation by administrators to assist in the negotiation process from time to time demonstrates the remarkable respect the County holds for Noridean McDonald. Her sense of presence in the workplace and her confidence continue to serve as a role model. It is important that an activist can find the union, but it is just as important for the union to find the activists within their ranks. Proof that one person can make a difference in the conditions of a workplace or an organization is exemplified in Noridean McDonald.

Many individuals have made contributions like that of Noridean McDonald, but most times they go unnoticed and under-appreciated for their efforts. I am fortunate enough to tell the story and the legacy of one of those many people. Noridean McDonald may not be a household name like Dr. Martin Luther King, Jr., Ms. Crystal Jordan (Norma Rae), Mrs. Rosa Parks, or Mr. Joseph P. Rugola. But her accomplishments need to be shared and embraced by all who believe in the united movement.

To others in the labor movement, I sincerely hope this inspires the many who are in the workplace and experience adverse and demoralizing situations. They should always remember their voices can be the catalyst of positive change, not just for themselves but for everyone. The only recommendations I can make to an organized structure such as a union is, if we do not remember our past we can lose our future. This project can be used as a union booklet for academic purposes to remind union members of the individual sacrifices and hardship that individuals have made to create a union to better the lives of workers across the U.S.

Let your people's voices be heard. Demonstrate and teach them by example. Dissect the merit of their complaints, and arm them with the tools of success needed to make a change!

"Laws can embody standard; governments can enforce laws—but the final task is not a task for government. It is a task for each and every one of us. Every time we turn our heads the other way when we see the law flouted—when we tolerate what we know to be wrong—when we close our eyes and ears to the corrupt because we are too busy, or too frightened – when we fail to speak up and speak out—we strike a blow against freedom and decency and justice" (Robert Francis Kennedy).

"The Litany of Thanksgiving"
Honoring
Noridean McDonald

It is the wish of many to serve humanity in a manner that leaves a positive lasting impression, but very few live up to the high demands. However, there is one impression in the person of Noridean McDonald who has left a legacy for the transportation workers of Cuyahoga County Board of MR/DD in Cleveland, Ohio, for whom we pause to give honor and thanksgiving for her service. To a lady who taught me that a tiny ripple of hope can bring down the wall of injustice, to you I say, "thank you with great admiration, love, and respect"! (Paraphrased from *The Litany of Thanksgiving Honoring Rosa Parks, 10-24-05*)

Your loving daughter, Davida Russell,
State Vice President, OAPSE/AFSCME Local #4/AFL-CIO
& President of OAPSE/AFSCME Local #744

Acknowledgments

To my family for their support in missing meals I did not prepare, for wading through stacks of books and papers while tripping over luggage, and for understanding my time absent from home. I would like to give a special acknowledgment to my husband Carl Russell for being my chauffeur to and from the National Labor College, for his support and encouragement through each and every class, and for all his time spent on this journey. To my friends and extended family, for missed quality time and for always saying I am doing homework when they would call or visit. To the Cuyahoga County Board of Mental Retardation and Developmental Disabilities as well as my own Local union OAPSE/AFSCME Local #744/AFL-CIO for their cooperation and support in helping me to achieve a degree. To my union OAPSE/AFSCME Local #4/AFL-CIO and AFSCME International for the financial support and the assistance provided to achieve my goal. To my silent editors, Kristen Schmidt and Kristen McKinley who unselfishly loaned me their skills and talent, to Ruth Ruttenberg who push me to excellence. Ms. Nancy O'Conner must not be overlooked. It was she who planted the seeds of further education and took steps to see that I had the necessary information to begin this exciting, compelling, and challenging journey to my future involvement in the labor movement. Regrettably, Ms. O'Conner is no longer with us to see the seed she planted grow. To God almighty for being the force that guides me.

Much thanks to one and all. Without your support and help, I may never have taken this road of furthering my education and spiritual development.

COMMUNITY TRANSIT SEkvICES, INC.

2121 West Crescent Avenue, Suite D • Anaheim, California 92801 • (714) 956-9830

File: C:Pers-McDonald

TO WHOM IT MAY CONCERN:

This letter will introduce Ms. Noridean McDonald who has been in our employ since August 14, 1976, and whose work record and attendance have been exemplary.

We regret losing this employee but due to circumstances beyond our control, in a competitive bidding environment, we are no longer operating the bus service.

We highly recommend Ms. McDonald for any position you might have available.

Very truly yours,

John J. Ford
President

EEA:nrs

PLEASE TYPE OR PRINT THIS FORM   ---   THANK YOU

CHAPTER OFFICERS REPORTING FORM

The following officers have been elected to serve OAPSE Chapter No. 744 of

Cuyahoga County Transportation School District in Cuyahoga County,

for the 19 79 - 80 school year. Term 1 year X Term 2 years _____

PRESIDENT

NAME Noridean McDonald

ADDRESS _____

CITY _____ ZIP _____

POSITION Driver

SCHOOL ADDRESS _____

_____

HOME PHONE _____

SCHOOL PHONE _____ EXT. ____

VICE PRESIDENT

NAME Barbara Harris

ADDRESS _____

CITY _____ ZIP _____

POSITION Driver

SCHOOL ADDRESS _____

_____

HOME PHONE _____

SCHOOL PHONE _____ EXT. ____

SECRETARY

NAME Marian Pearson

ADDRESS _____

CITY _____ ZIP _____

POSITION Driver

SCHOOL ADDRESS _____

_____

HOME PHONE _____

SCHOOL PHONE _____ EXT. ____

TREASURER

NAME Mitzi Stork

ADDRESS _____

CITY _____ ZIP _____

POSITION Driver

SCHOOL ADDRESS _____

_____

HOME PHONE _____

SCHOOL PHONE _____ EXT. ____

SUBMITTED BY: _____

TITLE IN CHAPTER: _____ DATE: _____

AMC
7/3/79

SUBPOENA

Appendix 3

UNITED STATES OF AMERICA
NATIONAL LABOR RELATIONS BOARD

To .... Noridean McDonald ....

....

Request therefor having been duly made by ___John F. Lenehan___

....

whose address is ....
................................(Street).............................(City).............................(State)

YOU ARE HEREBY REQUIRED AND DIRECTED TO APPEAR before ....

.....a Field Examiner........................ *of the National Labor Relations Board,*

at ....

in the City of ....

on the ___14th___ *day of* ___December___ ...., ___1979___, *at* ___10:00___ *o'clock* ___a.___ *m.*

of that day, to testify in the Matter of ....

C. B. Transportation Services, Inc.,..

....

....

A- 537236

In testimony whereof, the seal of the National Labor Relations Board is affixed hereto, and the undersigned, a member of said National Labor Relations Board, has hereunto set his hand and authorized the issuance hereof.

Issued at ....Cleveland, Ohio.....................

this ___12th___ *day of* ___December___................., *19*___79___

John H. Fanning

NOTICE TO WITNESS.—Witness fees for attendance, subsistence, and mileage, under this subpoena are payable by the party at whose request the witness is subpoenaed. A witness appearing at the request of the General Counsel of the National Labor Relations Board shall submit this subpoena with the voucher when claiming reimbursement.

Appendix 4

FORM NLRB-4279
(3-72)

RC-RM-RD

UNITED STATES OF AMERICA
NATIONAL LABOR RELATIONS BOARD

TYPE OF ELECTION

(Check one)

☐ Consent Agreement

☐ Stipulation

☐ Board Direction

☒ RD Direction

(Also check box below where appropriate)

☐ 8(b)(7)

C. B. TRANSPORTATION SERVICES, INC.

Employer

and

OHIO ASSOCIATION OF PUBLIC SCHOOL EMPLOYEES

Petitioner

Case No.

CERTIFICATION OF REPRESENTATIVE

An election having been conducted in the above matter under the supervision of the Regional Director of the National Labor Relations Board in accordance with the Rules and Regulations of the Board; and it appearing from the Tally of Ballots that a collective bargaining representative has been selected; and no objections having been filed to the Tally of Ballots furnished to the parties, or to the conduct of the election, within the time provided therefor;

Pursuant to authority vested in the undersigned by the National Labor Relations Board, IT IS HEREBY CERTIFIED that a majority of the valid ballots have been cast for

Ohio Association of Public School Employees

and that, pursuant to Section 9(a) of the National Labor Relations Act, as amended, the said labor organization is the exclusive representative of all the employees in the unit set forth below, found to be appropriate for the purposes of collective bargaining in respect to rates of pay, wages, hours of employment, or other conditions of employment.

UNIT:

All bus drivers, monitors and mechanics employed by the Employer at its facilities located at
                                    excluding all office clerical employees, custodians, and professional employees, guards and supervisors as defined in the Act.

Signed at Cleveland, Ohio
On the 10th day of March 19 80

On behalf of

NATIONAL LABOR RELATIONS BOARD

Regional Director, Region
National Labor Relations Board

46

APPLICATION FOR CHARTER   NO 744

Ohio Association of Public School Employees   **Appendix 5**

What is the potential membership in the school district or classification for which this charter application is being requested?

_____

Has an OAPSE Charter ever been applied for by this school district
or classification?   _____ YES __X__ NO

What Classification?_____

Does this request for a chapter charter arise from a consolidation
of school districts?   _____ YES __X__ NO

What are the names of the School Districts being consolidated?

_____

_____

Were these OAPSE chapters formed in one or both of the consolidated
school districts?   _____ YES _____ NO

What were the Chapter numbers?   #_____   #_____

Have the By-Laws of the Association been followed in accordance with
Section V - Consolidations?   __✓__ YES _____ NO

Is this chapter charter requested as a result of a division of classi-
fications of employees from an existing chapter?   _____ YES __X__ NO

Wht are the reasons for the division_____

_____

Pursuant to Section V of the By-Laws of the Ohio Association of Public
School Employees, we the undersigned, being not less than five (5) ac-
tive members of the OAPSE herewith request the CHAPTER CHARTER COMM-
ITTEE of the OHIO ASSOCIATION OF PUBLIC SCHOOL EMPLOYEES to authorize
the issuance of an official chapter charter to be recognized as:
Cuyahoga County Adult
Education _____ (XXXXXXXXXXXXXXXXXXXXXXXXXXXXXXXXXXX,
XXXXXXXXXXXXXXXXXXXXXXXXXXXXXXXXXChapter of the __Northeast__
District of the Ohio Association of Public School Employees. (Please
print or type the title as you would like to have it shown on your
charter).

The location of the proposed chapter will be at __Cleveland__
(City), Ohio and said chapter will represent the following school
district(s):__Cuyahoga County Adult Education Transportation Employees__

47

In making application for this charter, we hereby agree to conform with the rules and regulations and/or subsequent amendments as established in the Constitution and By-Laws of the Ohio Association of Public School Employees.
(Please print names of members below)

Noridean McDonald ✓	Crystal Mitchell ✓
Mitzi Stork ✓	Jerome Pannell ✓
Barbara Harris ✓	Clifford Cammon ✓
Marian Pearson ✓	Khadija Samipuok ✓
Wilbur Allen ✓	Shirley Williams ✓
Sharon Smith ✓	Addie Benison Collins ✓
Toni Loper ✓	Marguerite Davis ✓
Roderick Speed ✓	Ophelia Brock ✓
Princess Melton ✓	Ruthetta Patton ✓
Beatrice Jordan ✓	Beverly Goodwin ✓
Velma Walter ✓	Fred Thomas Jr. ✓
Idell Bunton ✓	Henrietta Parker ✓
Emory Phelps ✓	Deborah Mason ✓
Gwendolyn Ayers ✓	Walter XXX Venable ✓

Please verify the correct spelling of names by President's signature

Noridean McDonald President

AUTHORIZATION STATEMENT

By virtue of the authority vested in the CHAPTER CHARTER COMMITTEE in Section V of the By-Laws of the Ohio Association of Public School Employees, we hereby direct that a charter may _X_ may not ___ be issued
DATE _March 22_ 19 _80_

Liberty m Speters Chairperson

Field Representative Signature: _Karen Q. Huston_
or
Regional Representative Signature: _____

Chapter Charter

of the

Ohio Association of Public School Employees

WHEREAS, a properly executed application for a chapter charter of the Ohio Association of Public School Employees has been received and approved, we do hereby certify:

FIRST: The name of the chapter shall be ⎯⎯CUYAHOGA COUNTY⎯⎯ ADULT EDUCATION⎯⎯⎯⎯⎯⎯⎯⎯⎯Chapter No.⎯⎯⎯of⎯⎯CUYAHOGA⎯⎯⎯⎯⎯County of⎯⎯NORTHEAST⎯⎯⎯⎯District of the Ohio Association of Public School Employees.

SECOND: The place in this State where the principal office of the Chapter is to be located is⎯⎯CLEVELAND⎯⎯⎯⎯⎯,⎯⎯CUYAHOGA⎯⎯⎯⎯County.

THIRD: The purpose of this chapter shall be to promote the interests of public education; to advance the standards of the non-teaching school personnel; to help secure the conditions necessary to the greatest efficiency of non-teaching school employees and schools. Nothing in this charter shall be construed as taking cognizance of local problems unless a state-wide principle is involved.

WILBUR ALLEN	CRYSTAL MITCHELL
GWENDOLYN AYERS	JEROME PANNELL
OPHELIA BROCK	HENRIETTA PARKER
IDELL BUNTON	RUTHETTA PATTON
CLIFFORD CAMMON	MARIAN PEARSON
ADDIE BENISON COLLINS	EMORY PHELPS
MARGUERITE DAVIS	KHADIJA SAMIPUOK
BEVERLY GOODWIN	SHARON SMITH
BARBARA HARRIS	RODERICK SPEED
BEATRICE JORDAN	MITZI STORK
TONI LOPER	FRED THOMAS, JR.
DEBORAH MANSON	WALTER VENABLE
NORIDEAN MCDONALD	VELMA WALTER
PRINCESS MELTON	SHIRLEY WILLIAMS

IN WITNESS WHEREOF, We have hereunto sub-scribed our names this⎯⎯TWENTYFIFTH⎯⎯⎯⎯⎯day of ⎯⎯MARCH⎯⎯⎯⎯19_80_.

⎯⎯⎯⎯⎯⎯⎯⎯⎯⎯⎯⎯⎯
President

⎯⎯⎯⎯⎯⎯⎯⎯⎯⎯⎯⎯⎯
Recording Secretary

ACKNOWLEDGEMENT OF CHARTER

The Ohio Association of Public School Employees

Gentlemen:

This is to advise that the official charter for ___Cuyahoga County___

___Adult Education___, Chapter No. _____ of ___Northeast___

District of the Ohio Association of Public School Employees, dated

___March 25, 1980___, 19__, was received on _____, 19_80_

We will, at all times, honor this Charter and abide by the rules and regulations and/or subsequent amendments of the Constitution and By-Laws of the Ohio Association of Public School Employees.

Respectfully,

_____
Chapter President

_____
Chapter Secretary

(To be made out in duplicate. Signed original to be returned to the State OAPSE Office. Retain the duplicate copy for the chapter files.)

9/6/79
Revised
vei

April 1, 1980

Ms. Noridean McDonald
President

Dear Noridean & Members of Chapter #744:

Congratulations on your new OAPSE local. You have now
joined thousands of other members and officers who have
made this organization what it is today.

Since 1934, OAPSE has been in the labor business of re-
presenting school employees and we have learned a great
deal about the areas of greatest concern to you.

The OAPSE Staff will service and assist you in those
areas that are of concern to you and your membership.
You may call the

We wish you great success in your new venture. Support
and assist one another by taking an active role in your
chapter's activities. This will make your chapter strong.

Unity and participation are the main ingredient to make
your chapter a success.

Sincerely,

OHIO ASSOCIATION OF PUBLIC SCHOOL EMPLOYEES

Lawrence V. DeCresce
Executive Director

LVD:vei

September 13, 1982

Noridean McDonald

Dear Noridean:

This is your official notification that you have been appointed to the position of Bus DRiver at the East Side Garage effective September 1, 1982. Your rate of pay will be $6.91 per hour. Your hours of work will be determined by your unit manager.

Congratulations and good luck in your new position! If you have any questions or problems, please feel free to contact me.

Very truly yours,

John B. McLaughlin
Director of Personnel

JBM/kmc

Please sign both copies and return one for your personnel file.

_Noridean McDonald_____
Signature

1050 TERMINAL TOWER
FIFTY PUBLIC SQUARE
CLEVELAND, OHIO 44113-2286
(216) 241-8230

CUYAHOGA COUNTY BOARD OF MENTAL RETARDATION
AND DEVELOPMENTAL DISABILITIES

OFFICERS: Jane Kessler, Chairperson, Pedro Ilerio, Vice Chairman, Charles W. Duffy, Recording Secretary
MEMBERS: Glenn Billington, Peter J. Nemeth, Franklin L Sherman, Frank Kesler

Appendix

- Interview with Noridean McDonald (9/11, 12, 13, 14, 2006), retired first president of OAPSE Local #744

- Interview with Idell Bunton (9/11, 12, 2006), retired OAPSE Local #744 member

- Interview with Beatrice Jordan (9/11, 12, 2006), retired OAPSE Local #744 member

- Interview with Ophelia Brock (9/11/2006), OAPSE Local #744 member

- Interview with Karen Huston (9/11, 12, 2006), first field representative of OAPSE Local #744

- Interview with JoAnn Johntony (10/9,10, 2006), state president of OAPSE/AFSCME Local #4/AFL-CIO

- Interview with Louis A. Kish (12/1, 4, 2006), retired assistant operations manager for CCBMR/DD

- Interview with John McLaughlin (11/15/2006 & 12/14/2006), director of human resources for CCBMR/DD

- Interview with Roderick Speed (12/15/2006), former vice president and member of OAPSE Local #744

- Interview with Khadija Samiallah (12/15/2006), member of OAPSE Local #744

- Interview with Louis Johnson (12/28/2006), member of OAPSE Local #744

- Interview with Annette Washington (12/28/2006), member of OAPSE Local #744

- Interview with Barbara Harris (12/28/2006), first vice president of OAPSE Local #744

- Interview with Dennis Simpson (12/28/2006), member of OAPSE Local #744

Bibliography

Arlington Cemetery. (2006.) Retrieved October 11, 2006 from http://www.arlingtoncemetery.com.

Babson, S. (1999). *The Unfinished Struggle Turning Point in American Labor 1877-Present*

BLS. (2006). Bureau of Labor Statistics. http://www.bls.gov/.

Bollen, P. (2000). *Great Labor Quotations*

Canal, Lestudio. Enterprises, Regency. Alcoer Films. Warner Bros Studios (1992). *The Power of One*

Clark, P. (2000). *Building More Effective Union, Ithaca: Cornell University Pp. 71, 125, 190, 191.*

Dougherty, D. & Houston, K. & McDonald, N. (1980-1983). *Agreement between CB Transportation Services, Inc. and the Ohio Association of Public School Employees*

Donzella, M. & McDonald, N. (1983-1986). *Agreement between Cuyahoga County Board of Mental Retardation and Developmental Disabilities and the Ohio Association of Public School Employees*

Donzella M. & McDonald, N. (1986-1989). *Agreement between Cuyahoga County Board of Mental Retardation and Developmental Disabilities and the Ohio Association of Public School Employees*

Donzella M. & McDonald, N. (1989-1992). *Agreement between Cuyahoga County Board of Mental Retardation and Developmental Disabilities and the Ohio Association of Public School Employees*

Donzella M. & McDonald, N. (1992-1995). *Agreement between Cuyahoga County Board of Mental Retardation and Developmental Disabilities and the Ohio Association of Public School Employees*

Donzella M. & Russell, D. (1995-1998). *Agreement between Cuyahoga County Board of Mental Retardation and Developmental Disabilities and the Ohio Association of Public School Employees*

Donzella M. & Russell, D. (1998-2001). *Agreement between Cuyahoga County Board of Mental Retardation and Developmental Disabilities and the Ohio Association of Public School Employees*

Donzella M. & Russell, D. (2001-2004). *Agreement between Cuyahoga County Board of Mental Retardation and Developmental Disabilities and the Ohio Association of Public School Employees*

Encyclopedia. (2006). Reviewed October 15, 2006
http://www.infoplease.com/encyclopedia//laborbio.html

Green, J. (2000). *Taking History to Heart*

Goleman, D.; Boyatgis, R. & McKee, A. (2002). *Primal Leadership*

Hoyle, R.; Harris, M.; Judd, C.; Learning, T. (2002). *Research Methods.*

James, George G.M. (1956). *Stolen Legacy*

Jakoubek, R. (1989). *Martin Luther King Jr.: Civil Rights Leader*

JFK. (2006). Retrieved October 15, 2006 from

www.historical information/JFK.htmL.

Kennedy, R.F. (1966). Arlington National Cemetery Archives

King, M.L. (1968). *The Trumpet of Conscience*

Labor Biographies. (2006). Reviewed October 15, 2006

http://www.labor-studies.org/biographies.htm

Labor Relations Board, Cleveland, Ohio

Labor's Heritage. (2004).

National Labor Relation Board. (2006). Reviewed October 15, 2006

http://www.nlrb.gov/nlrb/contacts/contacts.asp

National Labor Relation Board: Achieves Library and case file

National Archives, http://www.nara.gov

NAL real. (2003). *Standing tall with a living legend*

Ohio Association of Public School Employees (OAPSE/AFSCME

Local # 4/AFL-CIO). (2006). Retrieved November 10, 2006

Parks, R. & Haskins, J. (1992). *My Story*

Quote land. (2006). Retrieved October 15, 2006

http://www.quoteland.com/author.asp

Random House New York. (1996). *Webster's Dictionary*

Renshaw, P. (1967). *The Wobblie*

Ryan, T. & Russell, D. (2004, 2007). *Agreement between Cuyahoga*

County Board of Mental Retardation and the Ohio Association of

Public School Employees and Developmental Disabilities

Santayann. (1863, 1952).

Siegel, B. (1992). *The Year they Walked: Rosa Park and The*

Montgomery Bus Boycott

Toffler, A. & Toffler, H. (1994, 1995). *Creating a New Civilization*

United States Government National Labor Relations Board

Unknown. The Washington Post. *10/26/05*

Witherspoon, W.R. (1968). *Martin Luther King, Jr.... To the*

Mountain Top

WVIZ PBS Broadcasting. (2006). Time Warner Cable. *American*

Experience: Eyes on the Prize, Ain't Scared of No Jail.

About the Author

Davida Russell, State Vice President

Northeast District President & President of OAPSE Local 744 of the Ohio Association of Public School Employees (OAPSE/AFSCME Local 4/AFL-CIO)

Davida's union activity began in 1976, with UAW Local 45 through General Motors. After being laid off from GM in 1979, she followed in her mother's footsteps. In 1981 Davida became a school bus driver for Cuyahoga County Board of Mentally Retarded and Developmental Disabilities (CCBMR/DD). After 12 years in the Transportation Department and as a union activist, Davida was elected union President of Local 744 of the Ohio Association of Public School Employees (OAPSE/AFSCME Local 4/AFL-CIO). Davida negotiated her first contract with CCBMR/DD in 1995, after graduating from Cleveland State University's Labor Relations Certificate Program. In 1999, Davida had the opportunity to serve nationally on President Clinton's Women's Round Table of Greater Cleveland and was invited to the White House on three separate occasions.

Davida's success has led to her greater involvement with union activity at the local and state levels. As former Northeast District Vice President, State Executive board member, and current Northeast District President and State Vice President of OAPSE/AFSCME Local # 4/AFL-CIO, she continues to represent more than 38,000 members across Ohio. Well known for her dedication to working people, Davida has been in the forefront of organizing, educating, training, increasing political awareness among workers, campaigning for pro-labor politicians and issues, and giving strong support on the picket lines wherever she is needed.

Davida actively holds leadership positions in several other labor organizations and OAPSE affiliates, such as AFL-CIO Unity Council Committee since 1994, International AFL-CIO Organization for Working Women since 1995, Coalition of Black Tradesmen Union since 1998, Vice President of the Cleveland Coalition of Labor Union Women since 1999, AFSCME International Health Care Advisory Committee since 2004 and the United Labor Agency School Advisory Committee since 2006. Davida is also an Executive Board Member of the Ohio AFL-CIO Labor Federation, the North Coast ALF Area Labor Federation as well as an Executive Board Member of the Cleveland North Shore Federation of Labor AFL-CIO. In this latter position, Davida has represented public employees in Sao Paulo Brazil at the URBIS 2002 International Fair and Congress of Cities where she received an award from the Ambassador of Italy for her outstanding work. Davida was entered into the 2004-2005 first edition of Who's Who as "One of The Most Influential Black Women in Cleveland Celebrating African

American Achievement". She has also been a co-host on a local cable public television show called "Another Look."

Davida has been featured in OAPSE's union sponsored radio commercials and in 2006 Davida wrote, produced and directed a union play called "We May Be Getting Old… But We Ain't Dead Yet"! The play was presented in Cleveland's downtown Music Hall for the 2006 OAPSE Convention.

Davida is a graduate of the prestigious Leadership Cleveland Class of 2004. She also graduated from the George Meany National Labor College with a Bachelor's in Labor Studies and in Union Leadership and Administration. Davida is a member of East Mount Vernon Missionary Baptist Church. She resides in Cleveland Heights with her husband Carl Russell and two daughters Domonique Nicole and Brittany Lynne Russell.

Printed in the United States
201077BV00004B/625-726/A